TOTALLY GROSS!

D1318100

Warning: Small parts may be a choking hazard. Not for children under 3 years.

ACKNOWLEDGEMENTS

Special thanks to Suzanne Cracraft, Emily Jocson, Jennifer Ko,
Maria Llull, Tami Sartor, Rosie Slattery, Lani Stackel and
Melissa Torok for their invaluable assistance and contributions!

Editorial Director: Erin Conley

Designers: Jeanette Miller, Lisa Yordy

ISBN 1-57528-920-2

Printed in China

{ 02 03 04 05 MP 9 8 7 6 5 4 3 2 1 }

TABLE OF CONTENTS

Introduction

I have always found it strange that children love to investigate gross stuff that has a real basis in science, but show little interest in learning the principles behind it. Equally perplexing is the fascination that most kids have with toilets and bathtubs. But again, the physics behind how water flows and how toilets work lacks the same addictive quality for most kids.

As a child, I was an exception. I loved anything gross whether it had to do with stuff going into my body or coming out. Burps, belches, sneezes and farts were some of my best friends. After all that, who would want to be around me?! One of my childhood idols was my neighbor's plumber, Bob Bompker. Bob would let me watch him fix a clogged toilet, clean out a sewer line or even replace a sink. He called me his junior plumber and when I was older and Bob was retired, I was the one the Michelsons down the street called to clear their drains.

Totally Gross was inspired by an offhand comment my wife made about kids not really learning science today—as well as the realization that I learned more science from Bob Bompker than from any teacher I ever had. Enjoy this weird, irreverent and genuinely gross science lesson—and please share it with the children in your life. They will laugh and giggle, but most of all, they will have fun learning.

Best regards to Mr. Bompker wherever you are,
— Bob Moog

Rules

Object

The aim of the game is to learn about science, get totally grossed out and have fun with your friends while collecting points.

Playing the Game

◆ First things first: grab a pen and paper to keep track of your points.

◆ The youngest player is the Reader for the first round and may not play until the next round. The Reader spins to determine the category to play (i.e. Sheep Burps; Boogers, Butts & Brains; Sour Milk & Black Holes; or Sickening Science) and reads the first set of questions from that section to the player on his/her left.

◆ If Sheep Burps was spun and the player answers correctly, s/he receives a point.

◆ Play continues in a clockwise direction, with the Reader reading the next player the next question in the category spun.

◆ After all players have answered a question, the person to the Reader's left takes a spin to decide the next category and is now the Reader for the next round.

◆ There is no penalty for an incorrect response.

Winning the Game

◆ The first player to collect 10 points wins the game!

Sheep Burps

Q: True or false: scientists are trying to protect the environment from sheep burps.

A: True! When sheep and cows digest their food, they burp a lot. These burps contain methane gas, which is a danger to our ozone layer.

Q: True or false: some bullfrogs are cannibals.

A: True. If they get hungry enough, they start eating each other.

Q: True or false: owls have no teeth and must swallow their kill whole.

A: True. Open wide!

Q: Which is good for snails to eat: sand, toenails or chalk?

A: Chalk. It has calcium, which snails need a lot of.

Q: How can an ostrich be deadly: if it pecks your heart out, if it sits on you or if it kicks you in the head?

A: If it kicks you in the head. It's got serious leg power!

Q: Are all snails male, female or both?

A: Both. Snails are hermaphrodites, which means they have both male and female parts.

Sheep Burps

7

Q: Is a cow's stomach bigger or smaller than yours?

A: Bigger. Nine times bigger, in fact!

8

Q: True or false: the largest earthworm in the world was 11 feet long.

A: False. One was found in South Africa that was twice that long: 22 feet!

9

Q: Which of these is not a reason slugs are slimy: to protect them as they move along, to make themselves too disgusting to be eaten or to help them see?

A: To help them see is the fake reason. The other ones are real.

Q: How many brains does a starfish have: none, one or five?

A: None. It has only a nervous system, which senses what it should do to survive.

Q: Which animal's sounds can you use to figure out what temperature it is: dogs, crickets or crows?

A: Crickets! For 15 seconds, count the cricket chirps. Add 39 to that number and the result will be very close to the temperature outside. How'd they do that?

Q: True or false: some cats can be healthy vegetarians.

A: False. People, and some dogs, can get the nutrients they need

Sheep Burps

13

Ω: Why do grasshoppers sing: for love, for war or for food?

A: For love. Grasshoppers sing to attract a mate. How romantic!

14

Ω: True or false: owls can turn their heads all the way around in a complete circle.

A: True. This helps them see from side to side, as they can't move their eyes.

15

Ω: How many times does a tick eat in its lifetime: 3000, 300 or 3?

A: 3—It must get really full when it does eat!

 Q: What do dolphins do while they sleep: swim in a circle with one eye open, make a bed at the bottom of the sea or float at the top of the water?

A: They swim in a circle with one eye open. That helps them watch out for predators.

 Q: True or false: boy aardvarks leave home when they grow up, but girl aardvarks just make a hole next door.

A: True. Female aardvarks tend to stay close to their moms. They even hunt for bugs together!

 Q: What do you call a baby fly?

A: A maggot. These wormy little larvae aren't such cute babies. They like to eat rotten things.

Sheep Burps

19

Q: What do camels do when they're mad: spit at you, pee on you or wail at you?

A: They spit at you. Watch out: that spitball weighs half a pound!

20

Q: True or false: termites can't fart.

A: False. Termites actually pass gas a lot—more than any other creature on Earth!

21

Q: What animal can eat a pile of sharp thorns for lunch: an orangutan, a camel or a pig?

A: A camel. Its rubbery lips and strong digestive system allow it to eat virtually anything.

Q: Where do dogs sweat: out of their skin, out of their tails or out of their tongues?

A: Out of their tongues. When dogs pant, they're cooling off by letting sweat evaporate off their tongues.

Q: What does a baboon do if it gets thirsty: lick the dew off its fur or get another baboon to pee in its mouth?

A: It licks the dew off its fur. A whole new meaning for "Do the Dew!"

Q: True or false: horses love to take baths.

A: False. Horses hate to feel wet, and they really hate the smell of soap. That's why they like to roll in mud after a bath.

Sheep Burps

25

Q: If a wolf made "scat," what did it do?

A: It pooped. Wolf poop and the poop of other wild animals is called scat.

26

Q: What do baby red-tailed hawks do with their poop: feed it to each other, spray it out of their nests or swim in it?

A: Spray it out of their nests. They can eject liquid poop up to three feet. So stand clear!

27

Q: People aren't the only ones who kiss when they meet. Which of these animals likes to say hello with a smooch: spiders, bats or chimpanzees?

A: Chimpanzees. They stick their lips way out and give a little peck.

Q: True or false: cows throw up their food, then eat it again.

A: True. They swallow it, let their enzymes work on it, barf it up, chew on it and swallow it again!

Q: Name two of the three things that all birds have.

A: Beaks, wings and feathers.

Q: What do slugs attack with: mucous, pee or vomit?

A: Mucous. When attacked, slugs use slime to fight back!

Sheep Burps

Q: True or false: all fish lay eggs.

A: False. Some fish carry their babies in a womb, like people do.

Q: Which of these creatures provided ink in the old days: deer, crows or squid?

A: Squid. Squid have ink they shoot out to escape from predators. It clouds the water, so the squid can make a clean getaway! People used to write with this ink.

Q: True or false: if a rattlesnake bites itself, it will die.

A: False. Mother Nature is too smart for that! Rattlesnakes are immune to their own venom.

34

Q: True or false: bees die every winter when it gets cold.

A: True. When it gets cold, the entire colony dies. Only the queen survives, burrowing deep and laying eggs to create the next generation.

35

Q: True or false: you cannot spot a boy elephant just by looking at him (in the same way you could a dog).

A: True. Male elephants do not have those easy-to-spot parts showing on the outside.

36

Q: Are those white splats birds hit innocent bystanders with made of pee, poop or both?

A: Both. A mixture of pee and poop go into those icky bird bombs.

Sheep Burps

Q: How does a horned toad defend itself: by shooting arrows out of its butt or by squirting blood from its eyes?

A: By squirting blood from its eyes.

Q: Is the horn of a rhinoceros made of bone, hair or mucous?

A: Hair. It's hardened, matted hair.

Q: True or false: the sewer rat can gnaw through lead.

A: True! Sewer rats will chomp through just about anything to get to food or water.

Q: True or false: most cats love to eat poop.

A: False! Dogs will eat it, but not cats.

Q: What keeps whales warm in the cold ocean water?

A: Blubber. These layers of gooey fat insulate the whale by helping it hold on to its own body warmth, like a sweat suit does for us.

Q: What do ostriches eat that you shouldn't: seaweed, hair or sand?

A: Sand. That's why they stick their heads in the sand—for a snack!

Q: What do elephants have at the end of their trunks to help them pick up food: bristles, fingers or tiny antennae?

A: Fingers! The Asian elephant has one and the African elephant has two.

Q: Do butterflies begin their lives as: snails, caterpillars or polliwogs?

A: Caterpillars. Before they take to the air, butterflies are crawly, hairy caterpillars!

Q: Is a turkey's second stomach called a giblet, a wattle or a gizzard?

A: A gizzard. You've probably eaten gizzard. Some grown-ups use it to make turkey stuffing.

 Q: Do electric eels really make electricity?

A: Yes. They use special organs in their body to make it. Shocking!

 Q: What's in a camel's hump: fat, water or another stomach?

A: Fat. The fat provides nutrition to the camel when it needs energy. If it gets used up, the hump shrinks.

 Q: Which of these animals gives birth by barfing up their babies: ducks, reindeer or frogs?

A: Frogs. The mom keeps the baby frogs in a sack in her throat. When it's time, she hurls them up like a corn dog after a roller coaster ride!

Q: What animal has a horse mom and a donkey dad?

A: A mule. If it had a donkey mom and a horse dad, it would be called a hinny.

Q: What fish can glide over water for up to 1,000 feet: the diving fish, the sand fish or the flying fish?

A: The flying fish. These fast fish can stay airborne for 20 seconds!

Q: What do cockroaches use to taste their food: their toes, their tongues or their butts?

A: Their toes. They have taste buds in their tootsies!

 Q: How do frogs breathe: through their noses, through their tongues or through their skin?

A: Through their skin! They drink through their skin, too.

 Q: Do any mammals lay eggs?

A: Yes. Two strange mammals lay eggs: echidnas and platypuses.

 Q: True or false: otters are known for their smooth, hairless skin.

A: False. Every bit of the little guy's body is covered with tiny hairs. Up to a million per square inch! They need all that hair to stay warm in cold water.

Sheep Burps

55

Q: If birds had a photo album of distant relatives, which animals would be featured: dinosaurs, crocodiles or frogs?

A: Dinosaurs! Scientists believe that birds evolved from dinosaurs.

56

Q: Can you milk a snake?

A: Yes! "Milking" a snake is a process used to extract venom. Experts use the venom to make a cure for the snake's bites.

57

Q: Silverfish will feed on which of the following: a book, a cookie or a live ant?

A: A book. These slithery insects love paper, so if you tell your teacher that a silverfish ate your homework, it's almost believable!

 Q: True or false: with a little patience, you can teach a goldfish to jump through a hoop.

A: False. A goldfish has a memory of three seconds. Sorry, goldfish owners, but your pet can't even recognize you!

 Q: Are there any vegetarian spiders?

A: No. All spiders eat meat. Some large spiders even catch and eat mice or small birds.

 Q: What do fish use for breathing: their gills, eyeballs or fins?

A: Their gills.

Sheep Burps

Q: Do fleas fly?

A: No. They jump. The common flea can jump up to a foot high!

Q: True or false: some animals eat the placenta (also known as the womb) of their young after the baby is born.

A: True. It is very nutritious and high in iron. Some people eat it, too—but not too many!

Q: Do dogs chase cats because cats run from danger and dogs like to chase anything that runs, or because cats smell like food to dogs?

A: It's because cats run and dogs like to chase. If the cat sits still, most dogs won't chase it.

Q: What is an owl pellet: a tiny owl poop that the owl eats again or a chunk of owl vomit containing the fur and bones of what it ate last?

A: Owl vomit chunk. No wonder people don't usually keep them as pets!

Q: How do dogs introduce themselves to one another?

A: They sniff each other's butts. You've seen it!

Q: What does an adult mayfly eat: its own head, toenails or nothing?

A: Nothing! As an adult, it lives for only a few hours (the shortest life cycle on Earth) so it just doesn't bother to eat.

Sheep Burps

Q: True or false: dung beetles collect and eat poop.

A: True! They even roll dung into a ball and lay eggs in it so their babies have food when they hatch.

Q: If you come across deer pellets, what are you looking at?

A: Deer poop. We call animal poop pellets when it's little and round.

Q: You've accidentally slammed the door on your lizard's tail and chopped it off. Will it remain forever tailless?

A: Nope. Many lizards have the ability to grow their tails back.

70

Q: True or false: most animals on Earth have a backbone.

A: False. Roughly 95% do not.

71

Q: What makes bees buzz: their flapping wings or a gurgle in their throats?

A: Their flapping wings. The wings are moving so fast that they make noise!

72

Q: Which of these animals can't have babies: the mule, the fly or the shark?

A: The mule. It cannot reproduce.

Sheep Burps

73

Q: Which of these things do dogs love to eat: vomit, poop or snot?

A: Poop. Something in poop is tasty to dogs, but we aren't sure what it is. And the dogs aren't talking!

74

Q: How do buzzards protect themselves: with farts that sound like gunshots or by projectile vomiting?

A: Projectile vomiting. When a buzzard needs defense, it shoots puke! Bonus gross out: then it eats it.

75

Q: What insect with a powerful sting glows under ultraviolet light (black light)?

A: The scorpion. Its hyaline layer has a mysterious substance that makes it glow.

Q: Who can mate once and be pregnant the rest of its life: the sparrow, the roach or the elephant?

A: The roach. Pregnant for life? Ask your mom what she thinks of that.

Q: Which of these animals eats by spitting its stomach out: cows, starfish or seagulls?

A: Starfish. It pops its stomach out, dissolves its snack, absorbs it and sucks that tummy back in!

Q: Is the lifespan of a dragonfly one day, one week or one year?

A: One day! These creatures only get to stretch their wings for 24 hours.

Sheep Burps

Q: True or false: if they needed them, flies could use one big contact lens, because their eyes are covered by one giant lens.

A: False. Their eyes are made up of hundreds of little lenses.

Q: Which of these animals does not give birth to babies: rats, pigs or turkeys?

A: Turkeys. Turkeys lay eggs. They're not born, they're hatched.

Q: What's the fastest fish in the sea: the sailfish, the shark or the zipfish?

A: The sailfish. One was caught going 68 mph. That's faster than you're allowed to drive on most freeways!

Q: What sea mammal has been known to eat fish, squid, seals, penguins—and sometimes its own kind?

A: The killer whale. No wonder they call it a killer!

Q: How many hearts does an octopus have: one, three or thirty?

A: Three. The octopus's blood doesn't carry oxygen as well as ours does, so it needs extra hearts.

Q: What can sting you even after it's dead: the jellyfish, starfish or stingray?

A: The jellyfish. Yes, its dead body can still sting!

Sheep Burps

85

Q: Which of these animals does not ruminate (vomit up food and then chew on it): a cow, a dog or a giraffe?

A: A dog. Many hoofed animals ruminate, including cows, giraffes, goats and reindeer.

86

Q: Which animal charted many U.S. highways: the buffalo, the wild boar or the horse?

A: The buffalo. Buffalo used to walk over a lot of this country and they picked smart paths. Then wagons used those paths, then we paved them... See how it works?

87

Q: What is it called when birds lose their feathers: molting, nesting or hibernating?

A: Molting. All birds molt in late summer.

Q: True or false: when a slug sheds its old outer layer, it eats it.

A: True. Aren't you glad you don't have to eat your skin?

Q: Which of these animals pretends to be dead when it is threatened: the cow, opossum or baboon?

A: The opossum. It will also drool and give off a stinky smell to steer predators away. Try that the next time you want to be alone!

Q: Are giraffes' tongues red and orange, black and pink or yellow and gray?

A: Black and pink. And giraffes use these long tongues to pull food from trees.

Sheep Burps

91

Q: True or false: cold-blooded animals maintain a constant body temperature.

A: False. Their temperature adjusts to their surroundings, unlike warm-blooded humans. That's why we need coats and snakes don't!

92

Q: What feeds on animals that are dead when it finds them: the crow, the vulture or the eagle?

A: The vulture. Its system can kill germs and diseases that dead animals carry.

93

Q: True or false: chimpanzees will eat other monkeys.

A: True. They eat mostly fruits and berries, but smaller monkeys are also part of their diet. So much for kinship!

Sheep Burps

94

Q: Rosie's friend, Jenny, told her that the turtle living in her back-yard disappeared for the winter. Rosie said that it probably went into hibernation. Is that possible?

A: Yes. Some reptiles do hibernate in the winter, just like bears do.

95

Q: Do snakes have bones?

A: Yes. Snakes' bones are just really small and able to move around more easily that ours, which lets snakes slither skillfully.

96

Q: What does a gecko do with its tongue: fertilize its mate, lick its prey all over before eating it or clean its eyeballs?

A: Clean its eyeballs. Unlike people, geckos don't have eyelids to keep junk out of their eyes, so they lick them like lollipops.

Sheep Burps

Q: True or false: for their size, grasshoppers are the noisiest of all animals.

A: True. They "sing" by snapping their wings.

Q: What does the African lungfish like to do in mucus: sleep, bathe or vomit?

A: Sleep. The lungfish wrap themselves up in a mucus cocoon and burrow in it for months at a time. Nighty-night!

Q: True or false: if a rat gets too hot, it will be soaked in sweat.

A: False. Rats don't sweat. They cool off through their tails and the soles of their feet.

Boogers, Butts & Brains

1 Q: True or false: kids grow faster in the springtime.

A: True! Though scientists still aren't sure why.

2 Q: True or false: if you have to burp but you hold it in, it will come out of the other end.

A: False. It will hang around until it gets the opportunity to come out of your mouth again.

3 Q: If you go to a doctor who is a proctologist, what part of your body is s/he going to examine: your feet, your butt or your tongue?

A: Your butt! A proctologist helps people achieve good health in their rectal and anal areas. Those are fancy words for your butt.

Q: Our bodies' waste comes out in the form of pee and poop. What form does plant waste take? (Hint: it's a gas people need to survive!)

A: Oxygen. Yes, fresh air!

Q: Which of these can cause bad breath: bacteria poop, tiny mouth snails or tooth dust?

A: Bacteria poop. The millions of bacteria in your mouth have to go, too! So, if you wait too long between brushings, the poop piles up.

Q: How much snot do you swallow every day: none, two cups or two gallons?

A: Two cups. That's the size of a carton of Ben and Jerry's ice cream!

7

Q: When an adult says s/he has heart burn, what does it mean?

A: It means that stomach acid has crept up the throat and caused a burning sensation.

8

Q: True or false: boogers are actually very clean.

A: False. They're full of germs! Their job is to collect the germs in the air and keep them out of our lungs.

9

Q: Why do we sweat?

A: To cool off. Sweating puts a little water on our bodies. As the water evaporates, it cools us off.

10

Q: True or false: you can't sneeze with your eyes open.

A: True. Try it! Maybe your body is protecting itself from all those tiny mucus molecules that fly out when you sneeze.

11

Q: On average, how much saliva will you produce in your lifetime? Enough to fill a toilet, a bathtub or a swimming pool?

A: A swimming pool! Yep, you'll produce about 6,000 gallons of spit in your lifetime, which is enough to swim in.

12

Q: Which of these is a symptom of bronchitis: runny poop, greenish mucus or burping up food bits?

A: Greenish mucus. Yup, green snot!

13

Q: Which type of burn will cause skin to blister: first or second degree?

A: A second degree burn will cause blistering of the skin. Ouch!

14

Q: If you get frostbite on your leg, will you have to cut it off?

A: No. Severe frostbite can lead to an amputation, but mild cases can be treated simply with warm water.

15

Q: What makes up most of your body weight: bones, skin or water?

A: Water. Humans are about 55-75% water. That's about 10-12 gallons!

16

Q: The word "lousy" comes from the name of a bug that can live in kids' hair. What is it?

A: Louse (which is singular for lice)

17

Q: If you yawn, can that make other people yawn, too?

A: Yes! We're not sure why, but yawning is contagious.

18

Q: Do people walk on two legs instead of four because of the way our spines are shaped or because our heads are so light?

A: It's our spine shape. It is shaped like an S, which is perfect for balancing over two feet.

 Q: Do we sneeze to push stuff out of our bodies or to help us see better?

A: To push stuff out of our bodies. We get the urge to sneeze when our noses sense an intruder or an irritation.

 Q: True or false: if you poked your brain with a stick, it would hurt.

A: False. Your brain does not feel pain. But the area around your brain would sure feel it!

 Q: True or false: cracking your knuckles could lead to arthritis.

A: True...this isn't just an old wives' tale. When you crack your knuckles, you inflame the joints, which can turn into achy arthritis.

Boogers, Butts & Brains

22

Q: Can your hair feel pain?

A: Nope. You need nerves to feel pain and hair doesn't have any. When something pulls on your hair, that pain is coming from nerves on your head.

23

Q: If you touch your friend's poison ivy rash, will you catch it?

A: No. Poison ivy isn't contagious. You can only spread it if you touch the sticky oil from the plant.

24

Q: True or false: farting into a thin, glass bottle will make the bottle crack.

A: False. But it can preserve the smell for several minutes.

Boogers,
Butts & Brains

25

Q: What metal do humans need in their bodies to survive?

A: Iron. We need it in our blood. We get small amounts of it from meat, fish and beans.

26

Q: Of the heart, lungs and kidneys, which have been successfully transplanted from one human to another?

A: All three. Imagine having someone else's heart beating inside of you!

27

Q: Can a boy and a girl be identical twins?

A: No. It's possible for a girl and boy to be twins, but not identical. They would be fraternal twins, which means they came from two different eggs.

28

Q: Which could you do faster: drink three liters of soda or pump three liters of blood through your heart?

A: Your heart is faster. It pumps three liters of blood every minute! Can you drink three big bottles of soda that fast?

29

Q: What is halitosis: boogers, bad breath or diarrhea?

A: Bad breath. In Latin, "hali" means breath and "osis" means disease.

30

Q: Name this pimple: a flat, dark spot made of oil and dead skin.

A: It's a blackhead. Kids usually don't get them, but when you go through puberty, watch out!

31

Q: Which of these is the medical name for the funny bone: fibula, humerus or sternum?

A: Humerus. When your funny bone is hit a certain way, it presses a nerve, producing a tingle in your arm. Humorous, isn't it?

32

Q: What is the scientific name for snot: dookie, mucous or puke?

A: Mucous. Yep, that slime pudding in your nose is called mucous.

33

Q: Do hair and nails keep growing after a person dies?

A: No. Skin around hair and nails shrink after death, making it look like these parts have grown, but they haven't.

34

Q: Is a lobotomy cutting off a limb, drilling into a skull, or removing part of an intestine?

A: Drilling into a skull. Lobotomy is a type of brain surgery thought to control violent behavior. It is now illegal in most places—what a relief!

35

Q: Your eyelashes work just like a certain car part. What is it?

A: It's the windshield wipers. Your eyelashes blink away goo, much like the wipers on your car clear away the rain.

36

Q: True or false: pink eye can be spread through things like makeup brushes and clothing.

A: True. If an infected person's eye drainage gets on these items, you too could wake up with an oozing eyeball!

Boogers, Butts & Brains

37

Q: Where are your smallest bones located: your mouth, your nose or your ears?

A: Your ears ... and you thought the only thing in there was wax!

38

Q: What condition is caused by a fungus that eats scalp oils?

A: Dandruff. Even if you don't have dandruff, you still have fungus on your head ... everybody does!

39

Q: Rabies is a disease of which part of the body: the skin, intestines or nervous system?

A: The nervous system. Rabies attacks the spinal cord and brain.

40

Q: True or false: popping zits is OK, as long as you only do it once in a while.

A: False. Popping a zit is like making a pimple factory! It forces bacteria even deeper into your skin, making more zits later.

41

Q: True or false: most people have as many jeans in their wardrobe as they have genes in their DNA.

A: False, unless you have one big closet! Humans have about 80,000 genes in their DNA.

42

Q: Drinking too much alcohol does the most damage to what: the liver, lungs or eyes?

A: The liver. Excessive drinking prevents the liver from getting blood to the right places.

Boogers, Butts & Brains

43

Q: True or false: giving birth underwater will cause brain damage to the baby.

A: False. Some women give birth in tubs of water. The baby breathes through the umbilical cord until it is taken out of the water.

44

Q: Do boogers protect our lungs?

A: Yes. The gook in your nose works like a net, trapping the bad stuff in the air to keep it out of your lungs.

45

Q: Which is not an effect of bulimia: stomach bleeding, rotten teeth or a swollen tongue?

A: A swollen tongue. But making yourself throw up after you eat can lead to rotten teeth and stomach bleeding.

46

Q: Can you bruise your brain?

A: Yes! It is called a concussion and it can happen if you hit your head really hard.

47

Q: Do doctors inject poison into their patients' skin to help them look younger?

A: Yes. Plastic surgeons give shots of Botox to get rid of wrinkles. Botox contains botulin, the stuff found in food poisoning!

48

Q: Some babies get greasy, crusty, yellow stuff on their heads. Is it crud head, cradle cap or crusty hat?

A: It's called cradle cap. It's dandruff for babies only, and it usually goes away on its own.

Boogers, Butts & Brains

49

Q: Name the two things on your body that won't make you scream in pain if they are cut.

A: Your nails and your hair. They have no nerves, so you can do whatever you want to them and it won't hurt.

50

Q: True or false: the left side of your brain controls the left side of your body and the right side of your brain controls the right side of your body.

A: False. It's the opposite.

51

Q: Melanin is a chemical found in what: your spit, hair pigment or toe jam?

A: Your hair pigment. The amount of melanin determines your hair color. Blondes have a little, redheads have some and brunettes have tons!

52

Q: Is there a difference between snot and boogers?

A: Yes. They're both mucous, but snot is wet and slimy and boogers are harder. Some people think it's funny, but it's not!

53

Q: Are incisors located in the mouth, the brain or the toe?

A: The mouth. Incisors are the teeth located in the front of your mouth.

54

Q: Which of these is not in your snot: germs, pieces of meteorite, fungi or none of the above?

A: None of the above. They all get trapped in your snot...even tiny meteorite bits from outer space!

Boogers, Butts & Brains

55

Q: Are the light-sensitive cells on the back of your eye called cups and cones, rods and cones or rods and staff?

A: Rods and cones. These cells send messages to your brain so it can tell you what you are seeing.

56

Q: How much does the human brain weigh: one pound, three pounds or five pounds?

A: Three pounds. Did you know that your brain stopped growing a few years after you were born?

57

Q: Which is not a symptom of a rattlesnake bite: difficulty breathing, foaming at the mouth or nausea?

A: Foaming at the mouth. But heaving and queasiness are common reactions.

58

Q: About how many times will your heart beat today: 1,000, 10,000 or 100,000?

A: 100,000. That's about 70 times a minute. What a muscle!

59

Q: True or false: you get tapeworms by getting mud in your mouth.

A: False. They come from eating undercooked or infected meat. Ask for your burger well done!

60

Q: Who has more bones: a baby or a grown-up?

A: A baby. Babies have 350 bones. They fuse together as we grow up, so adults end up with only 206.

Boogers, Butts & Brains

61

Q: How far do sneeze droplets travel before they land: 6 inches, 1 foot or 5 feet?

A: 5 feet! So cover your nose and mouth or be a snot sprayer!

62

Q: If you get caught in acid rain, will it burn holes in your skin?

A: No. Acid rain looks and feels just like normal rain. But in large amounts it's harmful to the environment.

63

Q: If someone has gall bladder stones, it means they are having problems: breathing, digesting food or farting?

A: Digesting food. The gall bladder's function is to help digestion.

64

Q: True or false: light can use your eye as a trampoline.

A: True. Light actually bounces around and enters your eye through your pupil (the black dot in the center of your eye). Boing!

65

Q: You got a polio vaccination when you were little. What does polio do: swell the brain, paralyze muscles or rot skin?

A: Polio paralyzes muscles. If it paralyzes legs, it makes people unable to walk. If it paralyzes the heart and lungs, it can be fatal, which makes the shot no big deal, right?

66

Q: What's cleaner: fresh pee or fresh spit?

A: Fresh pee. Pee starts out clean; bacteria grow in it only if it sits around.

Boogers, Butts & Brains

67

Q: Is it easy, hard or impossible to cure rabies?

A: It's impossible. Once a person gets it, rabies is fatal. The shot only works before symptoms appear.

68

Q: Is a scab damaged skin, dried mucus or clotted blood?

A: Clotted blood. It makes a sealant to protect the wound from germs and dirt.

69

Q: When a person has lice, about how many live lice is s/he housing: 12, 24 or 48?

A: 12. But that's live lice only, which doesn't count the possibly hundreds of eggs (or nits) stuck on his/her scalp!

70

Q: How much skin will you shed in your lifetime: 4, 24 or 40 lbs?

A: 40 lbs. Your body is shedding it all the time.

71

Q: Your body makes enough spit each day to fill which of these: a 1-liter soda bottle or a 12-ounce soda can?

A: A 1-liter soda bottle. Your daily saliva can fill that big bottle! Chug-a-lug!

72

Q: When you sneeze, boogers can hurl out of your nose as fast as: 5 mph, 25 mph or 100 mph?

A: 100 mph. If that booger was a car, it would get a speeding ticket!

73 Q: Your small intestine is filled with things that resemble teeny fingers. Are they called: villi, milli or vanilli?

A: They're villi, silly! Villi are like tiny sponges, sucking up nutrients from your food.

---

74 Q: True or false: the Bubonic Plague was caused by fleas vomiting rat blood into people.

A: True. Fleas drank sick rats' blood and got infected. Then they kept vomiting up the diseased blood while they were biting people.

---

75 Q: Which is bigger: the number of bacteria in your mouth or the number of people in the world?

A: The number of bacteria in your mouth is bigger.

Q: Is ringworm really a worm?

A: No. Ringworm is actually a fungus. So when you have ring-worm, you can say, "There's a fungus among us!"

Q: Why do people put chlorine in swimming pools?

A: To kill bacteria. If water sits around, it makes a lovely home for germs to grow in. You wouldn't want to dive into that, would you?

Q: True or false: it doesn't matter what kind of soap you use to wash your hands; they all help prevent disease.

A: True. Wash those hands with soap!

Boogers, Butts & Brains

79

Q: Did the Egyptians turn their dead people into mummies to preserve the body for as long as possible or to help the body decay as fast as possible?

A: It was to preserve the body. Egyptians believed that making the body last helped the soul last, too.

80

Q: Who poops more: you or a deer?

A: A deer. Deer poop as much as 20 times a day!

81

Q: True or false: your genes already know how old you'll be when your hair turns gray.

A: True! Genes are "encoded" with all kinds of facts about you. People are just now learning how to read some of these codes and learn more about themselves.

82

Q: When a woman says she is going to get a facial peel, does she mean she is going to put acid on her face?

A: Yes. A facial peel uses acid to remove the outer layer of skin, making the face appear smoother. Grown-ups are weird.

83

Q: Which of the following might be in your Aunt Edna's lipstick: fish scales, mold or beaver fur?

A: Fish scales. Cosmetics makers use fish scales for shimmer.

84

Q: Name two of the four blood types.

A: A, B, AB and O. Then there are positive and negative varieties for each of these types. Do you know your blood type?

Boogers,
Butts & Brains

85

Q: Which of these is not a common cause of farts: dehydration, undigested food or swallowing air?

A: Dehydration. Undigested food and swallowing air (like drinking soda from the can) both cause foul winds.

86

Q: True or false: if you eat a lot of asparagus, your pee will smell like asparagus.

A: True! It will be a little green, too. Try it...

87

Q: Name your body's largest organ.

A: Your skin! Skin is an organ, and a very large one—as an adult, you'll end up with more than 20 square feet of it.

88

Q: What is the hardest substance your body creates?

A: Tooth enamel. The hard shell around your teeth is tough stuff, and your body makes it all by itself (with the help of the right nutrients, of course).

89

Q: If you were to peel off all of your skin and put it on a scale, what percentage of your body weight would it be: 1%, 5% or 10%?

A: 5%. So, if you weigh 100 pounds, five of those pounds are just skin.

90

Q: Can the mumps be spread by sneezes?

A: Yes. The mumps virus, which makes your throat swell up like a balloon, is so contagious that it can even be spread by talking.

Boogers,
Butts & Brains

Q: Where does your body operate its chemical waste plant, filtering gunk out of your blood: your heart, your kidneys or your spine?

A: Your kidneys. They clean your blood and make sure it's perfectly balanced with the proper minerals.

Q: What is the purpose of the oils on your skin?

A: To make it softer. Sure, sometimes they cause zits, but those oils are really there to keep your skin hydrated and comfortable.

Q: About how many hairs fall off your head a day: 10, 50 or 500?

A: 50. If you kept all that hair, you'd have enough to make a wig in about four years.

94 Q: Do eyebrows serve a purpose or are they left over from our evolution from apes?

A: They serve a purpose. Eyebrows are shaped to keep sweat out of your eyes.

95 Q: True or false: most people's legs are different lengths.

A: True. Most of us have one leg that is ever so slightly longer than the other.

96 Q: When boys' voices start to crack, is that because their vocal chords are getting longer or shorter?

A: Longer. Until puberty, boys and girls have the same vocal chords, but then boys' vocal chords grow. While they're growing, they make weird sounds.

Boogers,
Butts & Brains

97

Q: Will gangrene make flesh turn green, become hairier or fall off?

A: It makes it fall off. If certain body parts don't get blood and oxygen, they can die and fall off.

98

Q: Where is the thinnest skin on your body?

A: On your eyelids. And the thickest skin is on the soles of your feet!

99

Q: If you want to buy shoes and make sure they won't be too tight, should you go shopping in the morning, in the afternoon or while you're asleep?

A: In the afternoon

Sour Milk & Black Holes

Sour Milk & Black Holes

1

Q: There are only two countries where you can find alligators. Name one.

A: China and the United States. If you live in the Southeast (especially Florida), you may have even seen one.

2

Q: Are volcano eruptions the hot insides of the earth spitting out, or ocean water and hot weather mixing together?

A: It's the hot insides of the earth spitting out. The hot liquid makes gasses that build up until ... bam!

3

Q: What makes a nuclear bomb so powerful: a chemical reaction inside the bomb or the force with which it is dropped?

A: It's the reaction inside the bomb. A nuclear bomb could go off without being dropped at all.

Sour Milk & Black Holes

4

Q: What travels faster than light: sound, rockets or nothing?

A: Nothing. Light is the fastest mover in the universe.

5

Q: True or false: peas are seeds.

A: True! Put a pea in the ground and water it, and you'll get a pea plant.

6

Q: What gives hot dogs their tube-like shape: dog tails, animal intestines or people's fingers?

A: Animal intestines. Hot dogs are made of processed meat that is pushed into the tubes of animals' intestines called "casings."

Sour Milk & Black Holes

Q: Is a cucumber a fruit or a vegetable?

A: It's a fruit! Simple rule: if it's got seeds inside, it's a fruit.

Q: True or false: Popsicles were invented by a kid who accidentally left his soda outside during the winter.

A: True! Frank Epperson was 11 when he made this mistake. When he grew up, he turned his accident into a business.

Q: Many household soaps contain which ingredient: animal fat, fish skin or bee poop?

A: Animal fat. Some soaps are made purely from vegetables. If you want to know which type you're using, check the label.

10

Q: Which one of these was not invented in the U.S.: the parachute, the escalator or the airplane?

A: The parachute. It was invented in France.

11

Q: Is the middle of the earth hot or cold?

A: It's hot. No one has ever been there, but scientists believe that the middle of the earth is 7000° F.

12

Q: What was invented first: the elevator or the bicycle?

A: The elevator. The first elevator was invented in 1852. The bicycle didn't come along for another 30 years.

13

Q: Is broccoli a root, a stem or a flower?

A: It's a flower. Hey, let's make a broccoli bouquet!

14

Q: Earth revolves around the Sun in one year. About how many of our years do you think it takes Pluto to travel around the Sun: 11, 125 or 250?

A: 250. It takes such a long time because Pluto is so far away from the Sun.

15

Q: If you have a pair of Levi's®, you know they're made of what: plants, animals or minerals?

A: Plants. Cotton is a plant! And cotton is the main ingredient of denim, which is what your jeans are made of.

Q: Which planet in our solar system is the only one that can experience a total eclipse of the Sun?

A: The planet Earth. Hey, that's us!

Q: Where do potatoes grow: in the dirt, in a bush or behind people's ears?

A: In the dirt. They're tubers, which are like root fruits!

Q: The first person in space was from what country: the United States, China or Russia?

A: Russia, which was part of the Soviet Union at the time (1961). His name was Yuri Gagarin.

Sour Milk & Black Holes

Q: Is the planet Venus hot and windy or cold and icy?

A: Hot and windy. That's because it's close to the sun.

Q: Which is the strongest metal in the world: gold, iron or tungsten?

A: Tungsten! Ever heard of it? It's used for all kinds of things, including rocket parts.

Q: How often does it rain on the moon: never, every year or every day?

A: Never. Actually, the weather on the moon never changes. No wind, no rain, no nothing!

Q: What causes tsunamis: heavy winds or earthquakes?

A: Earthquakes. Tsunamis start from an earthquake on the ocean floor that gets the water moving in one big wave.

Q: True or false: there is a plant that eats people.

A: False. The Venus flytrap does eat meat, but only insects, not people.

Q: Is a carrot a nut, a flower or a root?

A: It's a root. The green part at the top is the plant, but the yummy orange part stays underground, getting nutrients and water to feed the plant.

Sour Milk & Black Holes

25

Q: Does maple syrup come from bees, seas or trees?

A: Trees! Maple syrup is really the sap from a maple tree. Sap is sort of like the tree's blood... but, in this case, it tastes better.

26

Q: True or false: all volcanoes could erupt at any time.

A: False. Some volcanoes are dormant, which means there's no more hot lava pushing to get out of them.

27

Q: Why does peanut butter stick to the roof of your mouth: because it sucks up moisture or because it's full of air that creates suction cups in your mouth?

A: It sucks the water out of your mouth and soaks it up like a sponge.

28

Q: True or false: sunflowers turn around to face the sun.

A: True. They rotate very slowly to always face the sun. So if you want to know where the sun is, ask a sunflower!

29

Q: What makes milk sour: bacteria pee, bits of cow skin or milk worms?

A: Bacteria pee. When milk sits around, it starts to grow bacteria. And they have to pee somewhere!

30

Q: Let's say you and your family move to Venus for a year. Will anyone you know on Earth be here when you get back?

A: No, everyone you knew would be dead! One day on Venus takes 243 Earth days.

Sour Milk & Black Holes

31

Q: Does petroleum come from dead plants and animals, bird droppings or tree sap?

A: Dead plants and animals. Think about that the next time you go to the gas station!

32

Q: True or false: many Italian restaurants serve raw beef.

A: True! Carpaccio is raw beef cut into thin slices and drizzled with olive oil.

33

Q: What do solar cells need to produce electricity?

A: Light. Solar cells take that light and turn it into energy. What a bright idea!

34

Q: During summer vacation, you went for a hovercraft ride. What did you see when you looked down: land or water?

A: Water. Hovercrafts float over water.

35

Q: If you wanted to hike the highest mountain in our solar system, which planet would you visit?

A: Mars. The mountain is Olympus Mons and it's 17 miles high. Look out below!

36

Q: True or false: most living things in the sea are fish.

A: False. More than 90% of all living things in the sea are in the plankton family. What a big family!

Sour Milk & Black Holes

Q: Which country uses the most energy every year?

A: The US. We're doing better by conserving, but we still use more energy than everyone else.

Q: True or false: plants store energy in their muddy roots.

A: False. They store it in their leaves.

Q: Is the Mojave prickly pear a fruit tree, a cactus or a moss?

A: A cactus. And, true to its name, it's prickly! Its barbed spines can lodge in your skin if you get too close.

40

Q: Eating lots of beta-carotene (in vegetables like carrots) can do what: turn skin orange, turn eyeballs yellow or turn fingernails green?

A: It can turn skin orange. You'd have to eat a lot of carrots, but it can happen!

41

Q: Which is bigger: the moon or the sun?

A: The sun (400 times bigger!)

42

Q: True or false: when your cereal says "iron fortified," it means there are tiny bits of metal in it.

A: True. The iron breaks down in your stomach so your body can absorb it.

Sour Milk & Black Holes

Q: What is in the South American "chicha" drink: chewed up food, rotten rice or mill worms?

A: Chewed up food. Women chew pieces of the yucca plant, put it in a container and let it rot. Drink up!

Q: True or false: the holiday drink eggnog is made with raw eggs.

A: True. Eggnog is a mixture of eggs, milk and sometimes alcohol. It sounds gross, but people like it.

Q: True or false: if you screamed at your sister on the moon, she wouldn't hear you.

A: True. Sound needs air to travel, and there is no air on the moon!

46

Q: You are a world famous daredevil who wants to dive off of the tallest waterfall in the world, where will you go: Venice, Venezuela or Vermont?

A: Venezuela. The Salto Angel waterfall is over 3,000 feet tall. Better pack a parachute!

47

Q: What covers the surface of the moon: dust, water or clouds?

A: Dust. We think that the moon got hit with a lot of meteors once upon a time, which made craters and laid dust all over its surface.

48

Q: Where did carrots originate: Finland, Afghanistan or Brazil?

A: Afghanistan. Carrots showed up there thousands of years ago, but they didn't look like carrots today. They were purple or yellow!

Sour Milk & Black Holes

49

Q: Who invented popcorn: Native Americans, the French or the US Navy?

A: Native Americans. They showed the Pilgrims how to throw bits of corn onto hot stones. Aren't you glad they did?

50

Q: You just ate a whole hot fudge sundae. Eating what will reduce your chances of tooth decay: bananas, cheese or broccoli?

A: Cheese. So if you can't brush your teeth say, "Cheese, please!"

51

Q: True or false: air is held on the Earth by gravity.

A: True. Everything on Earth is here because of gravity: you, your house, even your dog.

Q: If an artichoke threw a party for its closest relatives, who would be invited: the palm tree, the daisy or the potato?

A: The daisy! Artichokes aren't the prettiest member of the daisy family, but they may be the most delicious.

Q: If you wanted to visit all of the mountains on earth, would you have to go underwater?

A: Yes. Oceans have lots of mountains, and even volcanoes!

Q: Where would you find a peanut: at the pea family reunion or the nut family reunion?

A: The pea family reunion! A peanut is a legume, which means it's a pod that splits in two. Isn't that nuts?

Sour Milk & Black Holes

55

Q: Which of these is the closest relative to our beloved vanilla: the lima bean, the tomato or the walnut?

A: The lima bean. Vanilla is made from dried beans!

56

Q: True or false: to navigate through space, a spacecraft must rely on the power of its engine.

A: False. Spacecrafts can use the gravitational pull of some faraway planets to help pull them through space. How nice of those planets to help!

57

Q: What do most desert plants use to protect themselves: pointy spines, plant fungus or bloody leaves?

A: Pointy spines. The pricklers in plants like cactus protect them from being snacked on. It's like armor for plants!

58

Q: True or false: giant kelp are the fastest growing plants in the world.

A: True. These plants can grow up to two feet a day in warm water!

59

Q: How long have people been eating grapefruit: 200 years, 2,000 years or 20,000 years?

A: 200 years. So folks were eating hot dogs and pretzels before they ever heard of grapefruit.

60

Q: On the moon, would you rather wear a coat or a swimsuit?

A: Go for the coat. But it still won't be enough! The average moon temperature is -292° F.

Sour Milk & Black Holes

Q: Is "broccoli" Italian for tree, arm or nut?

A: Arm. Maybe because it looks like an arm reaching out? Don't think about that when you're eating it.

Q: If you wanted to see a platypus at home, where would you go?

A: Australia. These unique mammals with duckbills live Down Under.

Q: Do 70% of all the almonds eaten in the world come from California, Cambodia or Kalamazoo?

A: California. And every single almond eaten in the U.S. is a Californian, too.

Q: True or false: earthquakes do not occur underwater.

A: False. And underwater earthquakes can form huge waves called tsunamis.

Q: What do people in Eastern Europe use to dye Easter eggs: tomatoes, oranges or beets?

A: Beets. Beets have a strong red dye. Ancient people even used them as make-up.

Q: Which of these is not recyclable: Styrofoam, glass or oil?

A: Styrofoam. It takes more than 500 years for Styrofoam to break down in a landfill. Uh-oh.

Sour Milk & Black Holes

67

Q: True or false: crabgrass gets its name from creeping into new territory, like a crab.

A: True. This quick-growing weed overtakes lawns by crowding out other grasses. So pushy!

68

Q: True or false: there is a plant that generates enough heat to melt the snow around it.

A: True! Skunk cabbage can do it. As you may have guessed, this plant also stinks.

69

Q: During spring break, you want to visit the world's longest floating bridge. Will you go to Seattle, Sea World or Ceylon?

A: Seattle. The Evergreen Point Bridge floats over 7,500 feet of Lake Washington.

Q: If sound traveling in air raced sound traveling in water, who would win?

A: And the winner is ... sound traveling in water! It's three times faster.

Q: Are the dark spots on the sun cool spots, hot spots or water?

A: They are cool spots. They're cooler than the rest of the sun's surface, but they're still blazing hot.

Q: True or false: cocoa beans taste a lot like a Hershey bar.

A: False. Chocolate as we know it has a lot of sugar added to it.

Sour Milk & Black Holes

Q: What makes a black hole: a dying star, a comet or a space storm?

A: A dying star. When a star runs out of fuel, it contracts, creating a gravitational field so strong it's inescapable. That's a black hole.

Q: Which of these can contain seaweed: lipstick, chocolate milk or ice cream?

A: All of them! Seaweed is full of nutrients and is used in lots of things. Thank goodness you can't taste it in all of them!

Q: Paper was invented in the same country that invented noodles. Is it China, Canada or Italy?

A: It's China. And these things were invented thousands of years ago, when most people in the world were pretty uncivilized.

Q: About how many volcanoes erupt each year: 50, 150 or 250?

A: 50. There are lots of volcanoes, but most of them go for years without an eruption.

Q: Cheese is most closely related to: liver, rotten milk or honey?

A: Rotten milk. Cheese is made of milk that is carefully fermented. It won't make you sick, though.

Q: Your school is having its field day on the moon. Will this help or hurt you in your quest to set a new high jump record?

A: It will surely help. The moon's gravitational pull is lighter than Earth's, so you can jump six times higher up there!

Sour Milk & Black Holes

79

Q: What is lava called before it spews out of a volcano: magma, crust or spud?

A: Magma. And it can get up to a blistering 2200° F. What hot stuff!

80

Q: If you want to take a romantic, moonlit spaceship ride, what two planets in our solar system should you not visit?

A: Mercury and Venus. They don't have moons!

81

Q: True or false: the inside of a cucumber is about 20° F cooler than the air around it.

A: True. It has a lot of moisture inside and is covered by thick skin to keep it, well, cool as a cucumber!

Q: Where did macadamia nuts originate: Hawaii, Australia or Honduras?

A: Australia. Hawaii is famous for macadamias, but the trees were imported there from Australia.

Q: What holds star clusters together: air, gravity or heat?

A: Gravity. These groups of stars are held together by a common gravitational bond, sometimes for thousands of years.

Q: You're going to the longest river in the world. Will you go to the Yellow River in Asia, the Nile River in Africa or the Amazon River in South America?

A: The Nile River in Africa. It's 4,200 miles long!

Sour Milk & Black Holes

Q: True or false: the only thing that can escape a black hole is light.

A: False. Nothing can escape a black hole, not even light (the fastest thing we earthlings know of!).

Q: Can you still eat chocolate that has turned gray?

A: Yes. Chocolate sometimes discolors if it gets a little damp, but it's still fine to eat.

Q: Which of these foods can change the color of your pee: beets, chocolate ice cream or chili?

A: Beets. You have to eat a lot of them, but, when you do, your pee will be pink. This is because beets contain a special red pigment (or color) that is easily absorbed.

88

Q: If a fly lands on your food, is it still OK to eat it?

A: No. Unless you like to eat fly vomit. Flies vomit all the time, so anywhere they land, there will be barf left behind.

89

Q: True or false: peanut butter was invented when a man accidentally dropped peanuts in his butter churn and had to grind them into his butter.

A: False. Peanut butter was actually formulated by a doctor as a high-protein treatment for his patients. It doesn't have butter in it.

90

Q: True or false: an ice cream headache (or "brain freeze") is caused by getting your brain too cold.

A: False. The pain is actually caused by nerves in your mouth getting too cold. You feel the irritation between your eyes, but it's happening in your mouth.

Sour Milk & Black Holes

91

Q: Do pineapples grow on trees, on bushes or on the ground?

A: On the ground. Pineapples grow on top of stiff leaves, which grow from the ground.

92

Q: True or false: the moon's Sea of Tranquility has more water in it than Lake Michigan.

A: False. The Sea of Tranquility has no water at all! It's a mare, which means it's actually a giant shadow.

93

Q: What do you call the frozen chunks of water that cover 10% of our planet?

A: Glaciers. Earth has so many that if you put them together, they'd be as big as Russia!

Q: What does NASA use to make space toilets for astronauts: the vacuum, survival of the fittest or gravity?

A: The vacuum. Without it, the lack of gravity on the spaceship would spread waste all over the place!

Q: Do any plants eat meat?

A: Yes. A plant called the Venus flytrap traps and suffocates bugs to absorb their nutrients.

Q: What are the white spots in salami: bits of salt, globs of fat or bleached meat?

A: Globs of fat. The animal's fat is mixed in along with the meat to add flavor and texture.

Sour Milk & Black Holes

Q: Which one is the closest relative to the mushroom: cauliflower, mold or dandelions?

A: Mold. Mushrooms and mold are both part of the fungi family.

Q: True or false: some people make omelets out of tarantula eggs.

A: True! You can get this delicious dish in some parts of Brazil. Yuck!

Q: Is root beer really made of roots?

A: Yes! It's made from the root of the sassafras tree or the sarsaparilla vine.

Sickening Science

1

Q: Which weighs more: the trash dumped into the world's oceans in a year or the fish caught in a year?

A: The trash weighs more. Three times more! And this garbage can kill as many as one million creatures every year.

2

Q: True or false: all poop smells bad.

A: False. Some animals' poop has no smell at all; some even has a good smell! Not ours, though.

3

Q: What has caused more deaths: all the wars in the world or mosquito bites?

A: Mosquito bites! Mosquitoes can carry deadly diseases like malaria. But don't worry ... vaccinations and cures have taken care of much of this problem.

4

Q: If you come across a bunch of bat guano, should you eat it, avoid it or catch it?

A: Avoid it. Guano is bat poop.

5

Q: Which of these is real: the sky apple, the sand celery or the sea cucumber?

A: The sea cucumber. It's a slimy ocean animal. Bonus gross-out: when a sea cucumber is scared, its guts pop out of its butt.

6

Q: When people say "14-karat gold," what does karat mean: the weight of gold or the percentage of gold?

A: Percentage of gold. Pure gold is too soft to make jewelry, so it is mixed with other metals. 14-karat gold is actually 42% not gold!

Sickening Science

7 Q: Which one of these discovered radiation: a grandmother, a married couple or a baby?

A: A married couple. Pierre and Marie Curie discovered radiation together.

8 Q: What is the temperature at which no molecules move?

A: Absolute zero.

9 Q: The next time you hear a telephone ring, you might think of its inventor. Was it: Thomas Alva Edison, Alexander Graham Bell or Benjamin Franklin?

A: Alexander Graham Bell. Does the name ring a bell?

10

Q: Is dry ice really a kind of ice?

A: No. It can freeze things, but dry ice is really liquid carbon dioxide. Real ice is solid hydrogen dioxide (also known as water).

11

Q: Is a sea sponge a mass of living cells that like to stick together or hunks of whale tongue that come off in its natural shedding process?

A: It's the cells that stick together. But the kind of sponge you use in your kitchen is probably man-made from plastics.

12

Q: Which one has a brain in its rear end: a newborn baby, a fish or a cockroach?

A: A cockroach. It has a "simple brain" in its butt that allows it to function even if its head gets cut off!

Sickening Science

13

Q: Which was invented first: the lawn mower or the zipper?

A: The lawn mower. It was invented in 1831 (without an engine). The zipper didn't come along until 60 years later!

14

Q: True or false: the two men who invented the airplane were brothers.

A: True. It was the Wright Brothers, Orville and Wilbur.

15

Q: Is a snowflake a chip from a large ice mass in the sky or a group of tiny ice crystals stuck together?

A: It's tiny ice crystals stuck together. That's why no two snowflakes are the same. It's hard to get all those crystals in the same pattern twice.

Q: In what way is an echo like a boomerang?

A: They both come back to you! An echo actually is a sound wave that bounces off of a large surface and comes right back.

Q: What habitat does mold prefer: a dark and wet place, a cold and flat place or a bright and dry place?

A: A dark, wet place helps it grow. Sunlight can kill mold. So open the curtains!

Q: How long have roller coasters been around: 350 years, 150 years or 50 years?

A: 350 years! 17th Century Russians rode wooden coasters over ice-covered hills.

Sickening Science

19

Q: Your friends Jeff and Vince are having a debate. Jeff says he saw a flying mammal. Vince says there is no such thing. Who is correct?

A: Jeff is right, as long as he saw a bat. Bats are the only mammals that fly.

20

Q: Your teacher writes with dead stuff! Yuck! What is it?

A: Chalk. It is made of plankton fossils.

21

Q: Dufus just peed on an electric fence. What happened: the pee bounced back on his pants, he got electrocuted or nothing?

A: He got electrocuted! Pee contains water, which electricity shoots through easily. That pee stream is like an electricity highway from the fence to you-know-where.

22

Q: True or false: a dad invented earmuffs because his kids were making too much noise.

A: False. A teenager invented earmuffs because his ears were cold! He thought of the idea and asked his grandma to sew them up.

23

Q: Is your anus a planet, the hole in your butt or part of your nose?

A: It's the hole in your butt. (Uranus is a planet, but "your anus" isn't.)

24

Q: What is another word for bacteria: grime, pollen or germs?

A: Germs. Bacteria is the scientific name, but we call some of them germs.

Sickening Science

25

Q: Does rubber come from moon rocks, animal hides or plants?

A: Plants. Remember that song about the ant and the rubber tree plant? Rubber comes from rubber trees.

26

Q: Who eats 500 pounds of food a day: humans, elephants or rats?

A: Elephants. You'd eat that much too if you had a 12,000-pound body!

27

Q: If stung by an Australian sea wasp, you have as little as how long to live: three minutes, three hours or three days?

A: Three minutes. This deadly creature is also nearly impossible to see in the water. Keep that in mind if you go swimming in Australia.

28

Q: True or false: raw caribou stomach is eaten as a dip.

A: True. Eskimos freeze, then thaw this stomach, clean it out and serve it as a smooth dipping sauce. Got chips?

29

Q: What Australian spider has a red dot on its back: the polka-dot crawler, the red back spider or the blood spotter?

A: The red back spider. And it can cause death with its bite. Yikes!

30

Q: Would a termite prefer to live in elephant poop, under car engines or behind gas stoves?

A: In elephant poop. Bonus gross fact: they also like to eat it!

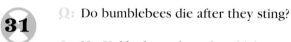

31

Q: Do bumblebees die after they sting?

A: No. Unlike honeybees, bumblebees can sting over and over again.

32

Q: Which mammal is the world's slowest: the sloth, the lemming or the pig?

A: The sloth. At top speed, a sloth will drag itself by its claws to move only 15 feet per minute.

33

Q: True or false: a dog's mouth contains special enzymes that make it very clean.

A: False. Dogs' mouths are full of bacteria. Think about it: a dog uses its tongue for toilet paper! Whether or not you let it lick you is up to you.

34

Q: True or false: a rattlesnake adds a rattle each time it sheds its skin.

A: True. A rattlesnake sheds about twice a year. So, if you want to know how old a rattlesnake is, count its rattles and divide that number by two. But do it from a distance!

35

Q: Can you train a guinea pig to use a litter box?

A: Yes. It takes a lot of time and patience, but it can be done!

36

Q: Is an animal that kills and eats other animals called an herbivore, a predator or a mammal?

A: A predator. Predators help our environment by eating plant-eaters. If they didn't, we'd have a shortage of forests and crops.

Sickening Science

37

Q: True or false: a donkey can see all four of its feet at once.

A: True. Get on all fours. Can you see your hands and feet at the same time? If you were a donkey, the way your eyes were set on your head would make it possible.

38

Q: What did some Native Americans use to start fires: charcoal, their hair or buffalo poop?

A: Buffalo poop! Dung is great kindling, because it's made of grasses covered with gasses!

39

Q: What might a female praying mantis do while mating: make a nest, vomit or eat her mate?

A: Eat her mate. A male mantis can still fertilize her without a head, so she bites it off. How romantic!

Sickening Science

40

Q: True or false: pet hamsters are descended from rats that were bred by English royalty to be furry.

A: False. Hamsters started in the wild, mostly in Russia and Syria.

41

Q: Are vampire bats real?

A: Yes! These bats drink the blood of their sleeping prey at night. Luckily, this doesn't kill the animal. In fact, it usually goes on sleeping.

42

Q: Which animal grows in its mother's womb for almost two years before it is born: the gorilla, the elephant or the dog?

A: The elephant. Baby elephants weigh about 225 pounds when they finally come out. It takes a long time to get that big!

Sickening Science

43

Q: True or false: a giraffe can clean out its ears with its own tongue.

A: True! You could do it, too, if your tongue was two feet long.

44

Q: True or false: elephant seals cannot swim when they're born.

A: True! Harbor seals (the shiny, little black ones) can, but the big, gray elephant seal has to be taught to swim by its mom.

45

Q: Who lays more eggs: the chicken or the turkey?

A: The chicken. A turkey will lay about 100 eggs a year, but a chicken will lay up to 300. They're both pretty hard workers, though.

Sickening Science

46

Q: What has warts: a toad, a frog or neither?

A: A toad. Its warts produce mucus to keep it moist, as well as toxins to protect it from predators. Slimy!

47

Q: True or false: the first gas motor engine was invented by a man named Otto.

A: True. Nicolaus Otto invented the first gas-powered engine in Germany in 1861.

48

Q: True or false: skunk spray is an ingredient in perfumes.

A: True. But the perfume guy would appreciate it if you call it musk, not skunk funk.

Sickening Science

49

Q: True or false: rabbits eat their own poop.

A: True. Rabbits produce two types of poop, one of which contains nutrients they need to survive. Yum!

50

Q: What do flies do most: barf and pee, shed little hairs or pass gas?

A: Barf and pee. Flies can only digest food they've already thrown-up. And they eat a lot! They also pee every few minutes.

51

Q: Which of these is the octopus's closest relative: the snail, the earthworm or the crocodile?

A: The snail. The octopus and the snail are both mollusks. Most mollusks have shells, but the octopus uses smarts to survive instead.

52

Q: Is the biggest cause of US forest fires human carelessness, lightning or fallen power lines?

A: Lightning. It causes about 20 forest fires a day. How shocking!

53

Q: True or false: pencils are hollowed sticks filled with lead.

A: False. Pencils are like a sandwich: two pieces of wood are glued together with graphite in the middle.

54

Q: Which has longer intestines: a human, a dog or a horse?

A: A horse, of course! If they were unwound, a horse's intestines would stretch for 90 feet. That's three times as long as a person's and five times as long as a dog's.

Sickening Science

55

Q: True or false: the bigger the goldfish's home, the bigger the goldfish.

A: True. In a fishbowl, a goldfish will stay just big enough to be comfy. But in a big pond, it can grow up to a foot long!

56

Q: The loop, whorl, spiral and arch are what: sea sponges, fingerprint shapes or marsh birds?

A: Fingerprint shapes. Everyone has them and no two people's are the same...not even identical twins!

57

Q: Which is in your Jell-O™: horse hooves, rat tails or fish eggs?

A: Horse hooves. Ground up horse cartilage is a common ingredient in gelatin, which gives Jell-O™ its jiggle.

58

Q: If your dad is driving at 55 mph, what does mph stand for: minutes per highway, miles per hour or momentum plus horsepower?

A: Miles per hour. So, at 55 mph, you would travel 55 miles in one hour.

59

Q: Can an electric eel give off enough energy to power a light bulb?

A: Yes. An electric eel can give off up to 100 watts of energy, the same as a light bulb!

60

Q: True or false: a male mosquito's bite is 10 times stronger than the female's.

A: False. Male mosquitoes don't bite. Only females do.

Sickening Science

61

Q: Did the man who invented potato chips also write the Declaration of Independence?

A: No. Thomas Jefferson wrote the Declaration of Independence. Chips were invented by a chef at a New York resort.

62

Q: A snail was recorded traveling 13 inches in 2 minutes and 13 seconds. What happened?

A: It earned a world record! That trip made Archie the fastest snail on Earth.

63

Q: True or false: without fuel, spacecrafts couldn't leave Earth.

A: True. Rockets get their momentum and speed from their fuel.

64

Q: True or false: ladybugs make parachutes to glide through the air.

A: False. Actually, spiders do. They make them from their own silk!

65

Q: Did dogs exist during the last ice age?

A: Yes. That means dogs have been around for a million years.

66

Q: Can a chicken get chicken pox?

A: No. The chicken pox virus is passed from and to people only. It's got nothing to do with chickens at all.

Sickening Science

67

Q: You squished a mosquito that was sitting on your dog's nose and red liquid splattered out. What is it?

A: Blood. Mosquitoes suck blood, so if you kill one right after it ate, you will probably see red!

68

Q: What do you think lives in a cow's stomach to help it digest food: bacteria, worms or a fish?

A: Bacteria. These germs break down food for the cow so it can get nutrients.

69

Q: True or false: there really is such a thing as a "bedbug," and it will suck your blood while you sleep.

A: True. When your parents say, "Don't let the bedbugs bite," they're talking about real blood-sucking bugs. But keeping things clean keeps them away.

70

Q: Is a fecal sac a poop container, a tumor or a scab?

A: A poop container. Many baby birds poop out into these mucous sacs, so mom or dad can conveniently dispose of the bag. Bonus gross out: they like to drop the sacs in swimming pools!

71

Q: What do you call the study of UFOs: ufology, alienation or rocket science?

A: Ufology ("UFO" = unidentified flying object; "ology" = the study of).

72

Q: In 1939, it rained more than just water in Trowbridge, England. What else fell from the sky: cats and dogs, worms or frogs?

A: Frogs! Strong winds carried the croakers up from streams and ponds and showered them on residents.

Sickening Science

73

Q: Does glue stick because it cools when it hits the air or because the water in it evaporates?

A: The water in glue evaporates. Then the sticky stuff can bond.

74

Q: True or false: after Christmas, you can take down the mistletoe and grind it into a tasty dessert.

A: False. Please don't! This plant can kill you if you eat it.

75

Q: True or false: Play-doh® was a cleaning tool before it was a toy.

A: True. Play-doh was first sold as wallpaper cleaner, but once kids discovered it was also fun to play with, the Play-doh folks made it a toy.

Q: True or false: scientists have no way to record the size of an earthquake.

A: False. Scientists use a seismometer to record earthquakes. This device detects vibrations in the earth.

Q: What is stronger than steel: a gorilla bone, the trunk of a palm tree or a spider's silk?

A: A spider's silk. If you compare a pound of the strongest spider's silk to a pound of steel, the spider silk is stronger. Five times stronger!

Q: For what did Mexican President Antonio de Santa Anna hold a funeral in 1842: his leg, his dog or his hat?

A: His leg. Bands played as the leader's leg was marched through Mexico City and taken to a shrine.

Sickening Science

79

Q: Every day, each person in the U.S. makes about how much garbage: 1/4 of a pound, 4 pounds or 14 pounds?

A: 4 pounds. That's about 1, 460 pounds per year. For just you!

80

Q: Nosegays, the little bouquets we know today, first became popular for what: covering garbage smells or curing colds?

A: Covering garbage smells. In the old days, there was garbage (and even poop!) on the street! People tried to block the smell with these hand-held flowers.

81

Q: How far does electricity move every nanosecond: an inch, a foot or a yard?

A: A foot. A nanosecond is one-billionth of a second. So if you raced electricity and took a step, electricity would have taken one billion steps by the time your foot hit the ground!

82

Q: Do seals grow up faster or slower than people?

A: Faster. Seals grow up in five years. It takes us much longer!

83

Q: True or false: an earwig makes its home in human and animal ears.

A: False. Earwigs live and hatch underground. Thank goodness!

84

Q: Scientists predict that the human population on Earth will double in the next 40 years. Will that give us 11 million, 6 billion or 12 billion people?

A: 12 billion—which means there are 6 billion of us right now!

Sickening Science

85

Q: Which was money in the days of Columbus: jellybeans, cocoa beans or pinto beans?

A: Cocoa beans. The people of Mesoamerica used them as currency back then.

86

Q: Do buttercups taste like butter?

A: No. Don't try it! Buttercups are poisonous.

87

Q: True or false: if you swim into a pool of piranhas, don't kick or splash (unless you want to get eaten).

A: True. They will also attack anything that moves if they smell blood.

88

Q: True or false: gorillas have more hair than humans.

A: False. Adult humans have about five million hairs on our bodies, which is the same as a gorilla.

89

Q: Which creepy creature helped establish the barber's red and white striped pole: the maggot, the centipede or the leech?

A: The leech. In the old days barbers also performed surgery using leeches. They took bloody bandages and wrapped them around a pole to advertise their services.

90

Q: True or false: dinosaurs are the biggest animals in the Earth's history.

A: False. Blue whales are larger than our ancient friends. And they're not extinct!

91

Q: True or false: all seashells have unique patterns.

A: False. In fact, all seashells in the same species have the exact same spiral patterns, like uniforms.

92

Q: Is household dust made mostly of bug poop, human skin or dirt?

A: Human skin. We're shedding tiny bits of it all the time. So dust is made of us!

93

Q: On which holiday do Americans consume the most hot dogs?

A: The Fourth of July. On that day, we eat an amazing 155 million hot dogs!

Sickening Science

94

Q: When you hold a seashell to your ear, what are you hearing: the sea, the air blowing through it or your blood?

A: Your blood. The shape of the shell sends the sound of your blood circulating back into your ear.

95

Q: What does your water smell like if there is sulfur in it?

A: Rotten eggs. The hydrogen sulfide gas in sulfur makes the water stink, but it's not bad for you.

96

Q: Does chewing gum come from trees, cheese or peas?

A: Trees. The resin of the sapodilla tree is the base for lots of chewing gums, although some are man-made these days.

Sickening Science

97

Q: Which of these will poison its neighbors: the black walnut tree, the red ant or the lobster?

A: The black walnut tree. It kills other plants in order to soak up all the water and nutrients for itself. What a meany!

98

Q: Which weighs more: your eyeball or 20 hummingbirds?

A: It's the hummingbirds, but just barely. Your eyeball weighs 1 ounce, which is equivalent to about 18 hummingbirds.

99

Q: True or false: Scuba divers' tanks contain pure oxygen.

A: False. The pressure of deep water makes oxygen poisonous, so Scuba air is mostly nitrogen.

Bonus Cross-Outs

1 Try to gleek.

Ever open your mouth to say something and have a tiny stream of saliva spray out? That's gleek! If you flex your tongue, touching the underside to the roof of your mouth, you can sometimes do this on command. It's really better done outside, though.

2 Pretend you're a monkey and groom the player on your left.

Are you doing a good job picking bugs off of the player? Monkeys do this not only to stay clean but to maintain close friendships, too.

3 Stand on one leg like a flamingo.

They do it to stay warm and to keep their feet dry. Getting tired yet? A flamingo does this for hours at a time!

4

Raise one eyebrow.

If you can do this, one of your parents probably can, too. The ability to raise one eyebrow is in your genes! You inherited this trait just like you inherited your mom's nose or your dad's terrible singing voice.

5

Cross your eyes.

Usually, this is easier if you extend your arm in front of your face, put a finger up, concentrate on the finger and bring it toward your nose. And, no, your eyes won't stay that way!

6

Check your toes for hair.

Some people are hairier than others. This has to do with age (people get hairier as they get older) and with your genes. Hair can show up in all kinds of new places. Check out your grandpa's ears sometime!

Bonus Gross-Outs

7

Swallow air by pretending to spoon it up and gulp it down.

When you feel the need ... and you will ... let out a nice big burp.
Wasn't that fun? Expelling gas is totally normal, and in some cultures,
a burp is polite! Ours isn't one of them, though.

8

Pretend your hand is the Blarney Stone and kiss it like you're supposed to: upside down!

Do it right and the Irish believe this smooch will bring you luck.
So make a wish!

9

Bite your bottom teeth over your upper lip and do an impression of a barracuda slowly swimming around the room.

Nice underbite! Those teeth can slice the barracuda's victims to pieces.
These big fish have huge appetites and may grow up to 100 pounds
and six feet long.

10 Show all the other players your belly button!

Is it an "innie" or an "outie"? This is the spot where your umbilical cord once was. Before you were born, that cord got you what you needed, like oxygen and nutrients, and it also got rid of your unborn baby poop!

11 Do your best imitation of a fly having a meal.

Ready to vomit? When flies land on food, they suck it up with their mouths and then puke it back out so it becomes a liquid. Then they slurp it up like puke stew! Eeeuw!

12 Check all players for eye boogers.

That yucky stuff in the corners of your eyes is made of sweat, tears and oil that drip into your eyes and are wiped into the corners by your eyelashes. You usually have more in the morning, because your eyelids were on break while you slept.

Bonus Gross-Outs

13

You are a deer tick sucking blood. Imitate what happens to you as you fill up.

Deer ticks are really small, but the more blood they suck, the fatter and more engorged they become. They plump up like a Ball Park® frank!

14

Smell your feet!

If your dogs are stinky, don't feel too bad. It happens to all of us! We all have little pores that ooze sweat from glands under our skin. Then, if the sweat sits around for a while, bacteria build up. Feet usually smell worse than other parts of the body, because socks and shoes trap the stink.

15

Pick your nose with your tongue.

Doesn't reach? Some people can touch their noses with their tongues, but if you know someone who can stick that tongue all the way in there, call Ripley's Believe It or Not®!

16 **Make a totally gross face by sticking your lips out as far as they'll go.**

Did you know that your lips are not part of your face? They're actually part of the inside of your mouth! That's why your lips are a different color than the rest of your face.

17 **Find the player with the smallest ears.**

No matter what size, all ears work the same way. They collect sound waves and carry them down the ear canal where you actually hear. Size doesn't help you hear more or less, but if you can wiggle them, that's just plain cool!

18 **Turn to the player on your left and look down his/her throat.**

See that dangly thing? It's called a uvula. We used to think all it did was hang around, but now anatomy experts think it keeps food out of your windpipe.

Bonus Cross-Outs

19

Pretend you are a female butterfly using your feet to taste the plant you're eating.

Butterflies have "taste buds" at the end of the tongue, so they use their mouths to eat; however, females taste by using sensory structures on their feet.

20

Show the other players your most visible vein.

Is it blue? Veins carry blood back to your heart. They look blue because the blood they're carrying does not contain oxygen, like the red-looking blood in arteries.

21

Show us your sideburns!

Your sideburns are the small patches of hair that grow along the side of your face in front of your ear. Boys and girls both have sideburns but boys may have to shave them as they get older ... unless they want to look like Elvis!

Totally Gross
Lab Experiments

Totally Gross Lab Experiments

Find one bug, inside or outside, and identify it. Good places to look: the corners of your ceiling or in the grass or plants outside.

What did you find? A spider? An ant? An earwig? These are some common bugs. There are a lot of bugs in this world. In fact, there are many, many more bugs than there are people!

Find a grown man and locate his Adam's apple. Now find a grown woman and locate hers. Is her Adam's apple too small to see or not there at all?

It's just too small to see. A big Adam's apple is what makes a man's voice deeper than a woman's. So that's what it's for!

Get a damp paper towel or washcloth. Press it on your arm and then wave your other hand back and forth over the damp spot. How will this make the spot on your arm feel: cooler, warmer or ticklish?

Cooler. This is how perspiration works! When you perspire, your skin releases a bit of water to cool itself. It's like your own personal air conditioning!

Take a piece of a brown paper bag and stick it to your forehead. Before you take the paper down, tell us what you think you'll see on the paper: wrinkles and rips, a dark spot or your name?

A dark spot is the right answer! The paper bag absorbed some of the oil on your skin. Your skin needs this oil to stay soft and healthy.

Totally Gross
Lab Experiments

5 Go to the kitchen and find some plastic wrap. Carefully remove a piece from the roll and wrap it around your hands. Will they get warmer or cooler?

They'll get warmer! This is because your skin is releasing heat into the air all the time. If you trap that heat with plastic, you've got hot hands!

6 Go in the kitchen and get a bottle of vinegar. Take off the lid and breathe deeply. But first, guess what is going to happen to you: your mouth will fill with saliva or your toes will curl

If you did it, you know—your mouth fills with saliva!

Spin around 20 times as fast as you can without falling. You're probably too dizzy to read this! Your blood got sloshed around. Does this make you dizzy because too much of it left your brain or because your heart can't pump it properly?

Because too much of it left your brain. Your brain needs blood pumping through it. Without it, you get the dizziness sensation.

Take an object, hold it straight out in front of you and let it drop. What natural force have you just demonstrated?

Gravity. Our planet has gravitational pull, which basically means that everything yearns to be next to its surface.

Totally Gross Lab Experiments

9

Go to the mirror and smile. Now point to your canines.

Your canines are your pointier "fang" teeth. Your big teeth and the ones on either side of them are your incisors. On either side of your incisors are your canines. You know what canine is a word for? Dog. Grrrr!

10

Get a glass of water and sprinkle some pepper in it. See the pepper floating? What will happen when you put a drop of dishwashing soap in the glass of water: the pepper will run from the dishwashing soap, the pepper will drop to the bottom of the glass or the pepper will stick to the dishwashing soap?

The pepper runs from the soap! And this isn't because pepper hates baths. What happened? The dishwashing soap broke the surface tension in the glass of water.

Find the player whose birthday is closest to yours. Have him/her sit in a chair. Hold your hand out flat and hit the person's knee (gently!) until his/her foot kicks up involuntarily. Is this kick called a spasm, a reflex or a tendon?

It's a reflex. This particular reflex is called the knee-jerk reflex, and it's really a kick! When you hit the nerve below the knee, it sends a message to your spinal cord, which causes the kick.

Spin around for 20 seconds and then try to walk in a straight line. Which of these parts of your body is making it impossible for you to keep your balance: your mouth, your eyes or your ears?

It's your ears! They carry fluid that helps you keep your balance. When you twirl around, you're splashing that liquid all over and it can't do its job.

Totally Gross Lab Experiments

13

Show everyone you're not ticklish by tickling yourself without even cracking a smile. What part of your body is preventing you from laughing: your brain, your fingers or your heart?

It's your brain. You can't tickle yourself. This is because your brain knows the tickle is coming. (After all, your brain sent the message to deliver it in the first place!) You need the element of surprise for a tickle that gets a laugh.

14

Show the other players the largest muscle in your body.

Better bend over! It's your gluteus maximus, better known as your butt.